God's
Top Ten
List

A Prescription
For Positive Living

Robert R. Kopp

CSS Publishing Company, Inc., Lima, Ohio

Copyright © 2001 by
CSS Publishing Company, Inc.
Lima, Ohio

Scripture quotations are from the *New Revised Standard Version of the Bible*, copyright 1989 by the Division of Christian Education of the National Council of the Churches of Christ in the USA. Used by permission.

Library of Congress Cataloging-in-Publication Data

Kopp, Robert R., 1952-
   God's top ten list : a prescription for positive living / Robert R. Kopp.
     p.   cm.
   ISBN 0-7880-1786-1 (pbk. : alk. paper)
   1. Ten commandments—Sermons. 2. Sermons, American—20th century. I. Title.
BV4655 .K66 2001
241.5'2—dc21
                                                          00-046841
                                                                 CIP

For more information about CSS Publishing Company resources, visit our website at www.csspub.com.

ISBN 0-7880-1786-1

To my wife
who
prays and works
to negotiate the delicate balance
between
law and gospel

(Galatians 5:6)

Table Of Contents

Preface

One of my favorite stories is about the pastor's son in his daddy's study. As a dedicated pro-lifer bends the ear of the pastor, he keeps saying, "You're right!" Then a rabid pro-choicer comes in to plead the case and the pastor keeps saying, "You're right!" After they leave, the boy says to his daddy, "They can't both be right." And the daddy says, "You're right!"

That story betrays the moral relativism or ethical exceptionalism of modernity. Or as someone said during a board meeting early in my ministry, "I know that's what the Bible says, but I think ..."

Everybody seems to be looking for exceptions to the rules — loopholes awarding the discoverer the license to do her or his own thing without regard to the expressed will of God as exemplified in Jesus and explained in the Bible.

But sooner or later, everybody realizes living outside of God's will does not enable wholeness, happiness, joy, and security.

That's what the following pages are all about.

God's Top Ten List explores the Ten Commandments (Exodus 20:1-17) within a Christological context not as a list of *do*'s and *don'ts* but as a prescription for positive and productive living. It's like my friend Tim Johns says, "The holier we are, the happier we are." Living within God's will is an opportunity, not an obstacle, to experience existential and eternal well-being.

J. Edgar Hoover used to say there would be no need for the FBI if people lived by the Ten Commandments.

I believe praying and working to incorporate this code of ethics into our lives will enable personal peace while contributing to societal renewal.

Maybe I should change the title of this book to *Ten Ways To Get What You Really Want.*

Certainly, honoring God will always yield benefits for others and ourselves.

1
One-Way Theology

"You shall have no other gods
before me." (Exodus 20:3)

God knows we don't do much theology these days. We don't try to understand and communicate the will of God as exemplified in Jesus and explained in the Bible.

These are the days of ideological navel-gazing in which "Well-I-think" rivals "Thus-saith-the-Lord" for sovereignty over life and ministry.

Everybody wants to paddle her or his own canoe, and spaghetti-headed opinion has been elevated to the level of intellectually credible reasoning and fact.

There are few examples more emblematic of this diabolical seduction — "You will be like God" (see Genesis 3) — than the religious universalism which has become so popular today.

Religious universalism is the silly notion that one religion is as good as another religion, and it's more a matter of personal preference than spiritual reality.

Loosely translated, religious universalism pretends it doesn't matter if it's Jesus, Buddha, Mohammed, Joseph Smith, Twain, Maclaine, or whoever works for you. It's that many-paths-to-the-top-of-the-mountain nonsense. It's a matter of taste rather than truth. It is rewriting Genesis 1:27 to read, "So man created God in his image. In the image of man, man created God."

Egocentrism is alive and well on planet earth.

But Jesus said, "I am the way, and the truth, and the life. *No one comes to the Father except through me*" (John 14).

Peter put it bluntly, "There is salvation in no one else, for there is no other name under heaven given among mortals by which we must be saved" (Acts 4:12).

Paul and Silas put it invitationally. When asked how to be saved, they replied, "Believe in the Lord Jesus, and you will be saved" (See acts 16:16ff).

Right about now, somebody usually complains about the *exclusivity* of Christianity. Balderdash!

Christianity is the most invitational and inclusive religion in the world. No other religion is nearly as class*less* and color*less*. It's easier to become a member of the Kingdom than it is to become a member of Oakmont Country Club. It's easier to get into the Kingdom than it is to get into a Steelers' game. It's easier to find a room in heaven than it is to find a seat at a Pirates' game. And you know how easy that is!

Or as Jesus explained the *inclusivity* of Christianity, "Whoever lives and believes in me will never die" (see John 11:25-26).

People who say Christianity is exclusive are just plain old ignorant. They don't know the facts. They don't know Jesus.

Jesus doesn't care who you are, what you've done, where you've been, where you live, or who you voted for in the last presidential election, though some people may have some explaining to do to him in the future.

The truth is everybody can get into the Kingdom through faith in Jesus. No other religion is as easy to access. Jesus doesn't fence out anybody.

Believing in Jesus as the *only* way, *only* truth, and *only* life is not an attempt to put down people who don't believe in Jesus. It is a faith statement that wholeness, happiness, joy, and eternal security will be experienced by anyone who trusts in him as Lord and Savior.

Exclusive? I don't think so!

Inclusive? Without question!

Quite frankly, I am baffled by people who say it doesn't matter what a person believes even after Jonestown, Heaven's Gate, and all of the rest. When people spout off about religion being a private and personal choice protected from the inspection of the church or state, I want to remind them that the same kind of reasoning freed gods like Hitler, Stalin, Jones, Manson, Khomeini, and too many others to do their devilish deeds. I just don't understand people who say it doesn't matter what people believe.

Belief is the foundation of behavior. And some behavior is hellbent. I just don't understand people who make allowances for hellbent beliefs and behavior.

But as we've already noted, these aren't the best days for doing theology.

Biblical literacy is at an all-time low. A Gallup Poll reported a few years ago that while most people cannot recite the Ten Commandments, they have seen the movie. It's like C. S. Lewis wrote in the preface to *The Screwtape Letters* (1961), "If you gauged the amount of Bible reading ... by the number of Bibles sold, you would go far astray."

Ann Landers recently provided a whimsical list which may reflect the level of biblical knowledge in today's world.

1. *Noah's wife was Joan of Ark.*
2. *Lot's wife was a pillar of salt by day and a ball of fire by night.*
3. *Moses went to the top of Mount Cyanide to get the Ten Commandments.*
4. *The seventh commandment is "Thou shalt not admit adultery."*
5. *Joshua led the Hebrews in the Battle of Geritol.*
6. *Jesus was born because Mary had an immaculate contraption.*
7. *The people who followed Jesus were called the twelve decibels.*

I think of the pastor who visited an irregular member of the church in the hospital. "I'm dying," the man said, "and I've got to know if God will forgive me for neglecting to worship and serve him if I leave a million dollars to the church in my will." "I don't know what the Bible says," the pastor replied, "but it couldn't hurt."

The notorious agnostic Robert G. Ingersoll asked Phillips Brooks to visit him in the hospital. "I appreciate this very much," Ingersoll told Brooks, "but why do you see me instead of your friends at the church?" Brooks answered, "I feel confident of seeing them in the next world. This may be my last chance of seeing you."

I recall the fellow who thought he could fly. He went downtown to Pittsburgh's Gulf Building and jumped off. As he fell halfway down, somebody yelled, "How are you doing?" He yelled back, "So far so good!"

As I think of the intellectual and spiritual dimness of people who buy into the New Age garbage about all-religions-being-the-same and it-doesn't-matter-what-you-believe, I cannot help but see that it *does* matter what we believe. It affects our behavior. And as those silly stories just illustrated, it flavors how we interact — behave — with other people. And as Christians, we know it's the difference between Kool-Aid and communion wine. It's the difference between dying in Nikes to hook up with the spaceship behind the comet and inheriting abundant and eternal life through the One who died for us. It's the difference between life and death. And if you check out history, you'll discover only Christianity has always chosen and guaranteed life for *everyone* through Jesus.

So don't tell me or delude yourself or poison people with the lie that it doesn't matter what we believe. It does matter. It's the difference between life and death.

If there is one way to wholeness, happiness, joy, and eternal security, why would anyone in her or his right mind choose another way?

The answer, of course, is in the question.

John Huffman, senior pastor of St. Andrew's Presbyterian Church in Newport Beach, California, recently told his congregation:

> *I am reading the recently released autobiography of Billy Graham titled* Just As I Am. *In it, Billy Graham describes his own crisis of faith. The year was 1949. He was preparing for a crusade in Hollywood, California. He had just had an evangelistic campaign in Altoona, Pennsylvania, that was, in his words, a "flop." One of his best friends, Chuck Templeton, had resigned his church in Toronto to enroll in Princeton Theological Seminary. Several times during the winter of 1948-49,*

he had talked with Templeton and discovered that he was having great doubts about biblical authority. Now, Templeton had come out to Southern California and joined Billy and several other speakers invited by Henrietta Mears to speak at the annual College Briefing Conference at Forest Home Christian Conference Center in the San Bernardino Mountains. Billy describes in his autobiography how, after the Altoona failure and his subsequent conversations with Chuck Templeton, he, himself, was struggling with doubts. Templeton had declared him to be fifty years out of date theologically. He suggested that Billy drop out of evangelism, go to the seminary with him, and learn theology.

One night, Billy took a walk out under those tall trees at Forest Home. The moon was out. He fell to his knees with an open Bible in front of him. There wasn't enough light to read that Bible, but he opened his life to Jesus Christ, promising God that he would teach and preach the Bible with the faith that would go beyond his intellectual questions and doubts. He would not claim to have all the answers, but he would preach the Bible as God's Word. He came out of that experience into the Los Angeles crusade and the subsequent decades of ministry in which he has been greatly used by God. Initially, Chuck Templeton was very successful, heading up evangelism for our denomination. Ultimately, his doubts about biblical authority led him to deny the deity of Christ, to leave the ministry, to become a talk-show host in Toronto, have a couple of divorces, make a stab at politics, and even to write a novel, cynically declaring that the Roman Catholic Church had found the bones of Jesus but had covered up the discovery so as not to lose the good, commercial thing they had going.

So I ask you again: If there is one way to wholeness, happiness, joy, and eternal security, why would anyone in her or his right mind choose another way?

The answer, of course, is in the question.

In *A Long Obedience In The Same Direction* (1980), Eugene H. Peterson addressed the benefits of one-way theology:

> *The main difference between Christians and others is that we take God seriously and they do not. We really do believe that he is the central reality of all existence. We really do pay attention to what he is and to what he does. We really do order our lives in response to that reality and not to some other. Paying attention to God involves a realization that he works ...*
>
> *God works. The work of God is defined and described in the pages of Scripture. We have models of creation, acts of redemption, examples of help and compassion, paradigms of comfort and salvation.*

That's what the first of God's Ten Commandments is all about: "You shall have no other gods before me" (Exodus 20:3).

God's first commandment establishes his sovereignty over our lives. "God," preached Dwight L. Moody in 1896, "will not accept a divided heart. He must be absolute monarch. There is not room in your heart for two thrones." Or as Jesus said, "No one can serve two masters" (Matthew 6:24).

That's why the Psalmist taught us to pray, "Give me an undivided heart" (see Psalm 86).

Clearly, concisely, and conclusively, God's first commandment spells out one-way theology: "You shall have no other gods before me."

That's the commandment.

Now here's the blessing inherent in the commandment: "If my people, who are called by my name, will humble themselves and pray and seek my face and turn from their wicked ways, then will I hear from heaven and will forgive their sin and will heal their land" (2 Chronicles 7:14).

Or as God promised through Samuel, "Those who honor me I will honor" (1 Samuel 2:30).

That's why John Huffman refers to God's Ten Commandments as *liberating limits*. In other words, living within the limits of God frees us to experience wholeness, happiness, joy, and eternal security.

I really like how the Reverend Eric Ritz explained it a few years ago in a sermon (26 April 1992):

> *Recently, the Sunday school class that I am teaching examined the Ten Commandments and why they were given by God to Moses. They were given to Moses as he led the nation of Israel to the Promised Land. We discovered they were not given by an angry God who wanted to deny freedom and joy to his people. They were given by a loving God to instruct his people to say, "No," to one way of life in order to say, "Yes," to a greater way of life.*

Simply, God's sovereignty saves us here and now and forever.

When my son was in seventh grade, he didn't want to play football. I said I wouldn't feed him unless he played. He played.

When he said he didn't want to wrestle, I said I wouldn't feed him unless he wrestled. He wrestled.

When he said he didn't want to go out for track and field, I said I wouldn't feed him unless he went out for track and field. He went out for track and field.

Aside from the less than subtle message that I'm trying to convey about parental responsibility to those parents who seem to forget the difference between being an adult and a child, I mention this because I was convinced back then and remain convinced now that most parents know a lot more about what children need to succeed than children. Children need parents to exercise a lot of parental prerogative — teaching them right from wrong and making choices for them until they reach emotional, intellectual, and spiritual maturity — in order to survive the perils of childhood and temptations of youth.

Similarly, one-way theology is a blessing rather than a burden. It is an opportunity to experience God's best by being our best for God.

So if there is one way to wholeness, happiness, joy, and eternal security, why would anyone in her or his right mind choose another way?

The answer, of course, is in the question.

That's what the first of God's Ten Commandments is all about.

Let me put it another way.

Father knows best.

2
Dime Store Faith

*"You shall not make for yourself
an idol." (Exodus 20:4)*

Growing up in a little town which nobody has heard of across the Susquehanna River from Wilkes-Barre, Pennsylvania, our family attended the Forty Fort United Presbyterian Church.

I have so many warm and encouraging and reassuring memories from that church.

I guess that's a big part of why I tell parents who want their babies baptized to keep their promise about bringing up children in the nurture and admonition of the Lord so they aren't deprived of the joys and excitement and security of Christmas, Easter, Sunday school, picnics, Vacation Bible School, musical programs, youth groups, and all of the rest.

Anyway, I've got great memories from Forty Fort.

My 103-year-old Sunday school teacher Grace Blanchard who insisted on teaching only boys began the first class of every month by saying, "Today, it's S-O-S! Same old stuff!"

Then there was Helen Kobusky. I'll never forget that hayride. And to think some kids don't like youth group.

Scouts met in the church.

Miss Jones — our school's guidance counselor who also taught Sunday school and ran the Yankee Youth Center on Friday nights and made prison wardens look like sissies — always made us practice our parts for the annual Christmas Eve service in the sanctuary in front of her. I can still hear her yelling, "Enunciate, Bobby Kopp, *enunciate!*"

David Meeker and I — members of Boy Scout Troop 122 — would always chase Mark Tedrow — a member of Boy Scout Troop 123 — home in a Christian kind of way after meeting with Pastor Mante to work on our God and Country awards.

17

I remember the Reverend Harold F. Mante who will always be my model for ministry in the spirit of αγαπη love. He knew the bad and ugly about everybody but always concentrated on the good in and possible for everybody.

But most of all, I remember sitting in worship with Mom, Dad, Grandma Thelma, and Sister Sue. Long before it became a popular phrase and now long after the phrase has become tired, I experienced the blessed truth that families that pray together stay together.

There's one other memory that kind of bothers me.

My parents used to give me a dollar for "the collection." I used to give God his cut or tithe and spend the rest at the dime store.

And now that many years have passed, I've come to realize the stuff that I bought at the dime store hasn't lasted as long as what I heard and learned and experienced in that old Forty Fort United Presbyterian Church.

Too many of us get sucked into dime store faith. We place our confidence in people and things that are cheap and wear out.

Consider the futility of our fascination with heroes. Hero worship is the real fatal attraction of the generations:

— Adam and Eve didn't stick to their diets.

— Moses couldn't cover up a murder or bad temper.

— Samson's strength was no match for the seductions of Delilah.

— David remains the greatest king in the history of Israel, but he had zipper problems.

— Thomas Jefferson could really write about life and liberty while enslaving people.

— Babe Ruth struck out a lot more than he hit.

— Mickey Mantle was a drunk.

— Joe Namath wore panty hose.

— Michael's gone.

— Mike Tyson bit off more than he can chew.

— And before the blinking of a newsman, we find out Evander Holyfield also bit an opponent and has six children by six different women.

— Tiger Woods can't win every week.

— Nobody's a favorite with the fans at Three Rivers Stadium for very long.

Ralph Waldo Emerson was right. He said, "Every hero becomes at last a bore."

And it doesn't help when I get up in the morning, look in the mirror, and don't shave. How about you?

When I turned 47, a friend called and said, "Life begins at 45! Then it's patch, patch, patch!" It's too bad we can't cover up our humanity.

That's why God gave us the second of his commandments: "You shall not make for yourself an idol."

It's a simple commandment. God commands rejection of anyone or anything that gets in the way of communion with him.

Martin Luther explained it this way in *The Large Catechism* (1529): "God will tolerate no presumption and no trust in any other object. He makes no greater demand on us than a hearty trust in him for all blessings."

It's a prohibition against "I-don't-care-if-it-rains-or-freezes-as-long-as-I've-got-my-plastic-Jesus-right-on-the-dashboard-of-my-car" religion.

Just in case anyone assumes our Lord is being a little picky about folks who get into brass plaques, dashboard deities, sports shoe superstars, and other kinds of hero worship, the commandment is a warning against placing trust in the untrustworthy.

The problem with human heroes and "carved idols" is that they don't work. They don't satisfy. They're cheap. They wear out. They don't save. "Whatever we may say about God," Augustine said, "no words or pictures or monuments or whatever will ever come within reach of his dignity." Or as Walter Harrelson wrote in *The Ten Commandments and Human Rights* (1980), "The commandment insists that there is in fact no reality on earth that suffices to provide the representation of Deity."

That's why Paul so mockingly addressed the people in the middle of the Areopagus, "Men of Athens, I perceive that in every way you are very religious. For as I passed along, and observed the objects of your worship, I found an altar with this inscription, 'To an unknown God' " (see Acts 17:16ff).

19

In other words, it's a waste of time, effort, and emotion to look to anyone or anything for what only our Lord can provide. It's dime store faith. It's cheap. It wears out. It doesn't work. It doesn't save.

God's people have found the truth in this old world. And it isn't dime store faith. *He's Jesus!* The knowledge of God in Jesus hangs around our necks like pearls instead of chains.

Ralph Earle, the great biblical scholar who taught at Kansas City's Nazarene Theological Seminary and helped edit *The New International Version* of the Bible, often told the story of John G. Paton who was a pioneer missionary to the New Hebrides. Dr. Paton soon discovered that while the natives had words for house, tree, stone, and the like, they had no words for love, joy, and peace. Worst of all, they had no word for believe. One day as he sat in his hut filled with frustration, an old native entered and slumped down in a chair. Exhausted from a long journey, the man said, "I'm leaning my whole weight on this chair." "What did you say?" asked Dr. Paton. "I'm leaning," the man repeated, "my whole weight on this chair." Immediately, Dr. Paton cried, "That's it!" And from that day forward for that primitive tribe, "Believe in Jesus" became "Lean your whole weight on Jesus."

That's what this commandment is all about. It's about leaning on God — *trusting him* — for existential and eternal security. No one nor thing can support us like our Lord. There are no substitutes for his ability. Therefore, there are no substitutes for the attention, affection, and allegiance due him alone.

Frederick Buechner put it this way in *Wishful Thinking* (1973):

> *Idolatry is the practice of ascribing absolute value to things of relative worth. Under certain circumstances money, patriotism, sexual freedom, moral principles, family loyalty, physical health, social, or intellectual preeminence, and so on are fine things to have around, but to make them your masters, to look to them to justify your life and save your soul is sheerest folly. They just aren't up to it.*

But *Jesus* is!
Praise God!

20

3
Putting Words In His Mouth

"You shall not make wrongful use of the name of the Lord your God." (Exodus 20:7)

Standing in the express line at Shop N' Spend can test one's soul, especially if the person just in front of you has 46 items over the limit and wants to use a check but forgot to bring the driver's license.

So it's not uncommon to scan the tabloids to see how Oprah is doing on her diet, or if our Congressman has been messing around with somebody, or why our favorite sneaker corporation says it's okay to pay five cents an hour to eight year olds in Haiti, or when JFK or Elvis appeared at the mall in Newport Beach to tell us when Jesus is coming back.

But here's a line that really caught my attention the other day: "Will shaving against the grain make hair grow back tougher?"

I've learned three things about bald guys: (1) you never know for sure; (2) they always carry combs; and (3) anything written or said about hair captivates them.

Of course, the hair line appeared just below this question: "Does eating chocolate give you zits?"

Those are the kinds of thoughts that help pass time in traffic jams at Shop N' Spend's express line.

Actually, those lines are on the cover of Sue Castle's *The Truth About Old Wives' Tales* (1997). And when the checker decided to call for the manager to get clearance for the licenseless checkwriter in front of me with 46 items, I decided to pick it off the rack and buy it.

Parenthetically, I know men tell old guys' tales. You know those fish size and golf score and Bruce Springsteen "Glory Days" stories. But this book was about old wives' tales.

The author began:

21

On a news show the other morning, in response to one guest's remark, the host asked, "Is that true, or is it just another old wives' tale?" Why is the received wisdom of the ages so often dismissed in such a cavalier manner? Are all old wives' tales automatically thought of as nonsense? ... Are all old wives' tales just so much superstitious nonsense, or is there much more to them than that? Is there a grain of truth to any of them? ... Join me now in a fact or fiction mission of some of the best known old wives' tales.

It's important to know true from false.

Just after being ordained, I moderated my first session meeting at the First United Presbyterian Church of Parkesburg, Pennsylvania. After outlining a renewal program for the sleepy little church, an elder looked at me and said without charity, "Are you crazy? We aren't going to do any of that!"

Ah, the simple joys of ministry.

Not long after that, I visited Viola Hawk. She was an elder. She asked me to baptize her Scottish terrier.

Aside from being one of the first clues that our denomination is in a serious theological crisis, it also taught me that it's important to know true from false.

But how can we know the difference? Specifically, how can we know the will of God?

God's people have always understood his will within the context of the example of Jesus, the Bible, the Church's confessions, and the enlightenment of the Holy Spirit.

Jerry Kirk, President of the National Coalition Against Pornography and former senior pastor of Cincinnati's College Hill Presbyterian Church, explained it this way to me: "We are called to be and do everything our Lord has called us to be and do as exemplified in Jesus and explained in the Bible."

The Confession of 1967 is precise:

> *Confessions and declarations are subordinate standards in the church ... subject to the authority of Jesus Christ, the Word of God, as the Scriptures bear witness to him.*

22

No one type of confession is exclusively valid, no one standard is irreformable. Obedience to Jesus Christ alone identifies the one universal Church and supplies the continuity of its traditions.

In other words, any creed or deed that *contradicts* God's will as exemplified in Jesus and explained in the Bible even if it comes from the church or people who claim to be God's *must* be rejected. But any creed or deed that *conforms* to God's will as exemplified in Jesus and explained in the Bible must be embraced by the church and people who claim to be God's.

It's the only Christian thing to do.

Knowing God's will — knowing the difference between true and false or knowing the difference between autosuggestion and the Word of God — is what God's third commandment is all about: "You shall not make wrongful use of the name of the Lord your God" (Exodus 20:7).

Essentially, this commandment prohibits ascribing anything to God or assuming anything about God that is not consistent with the example of Jesus and witness of the Bible. To attach God's name (i.e., his being and character) to anything that is not true within this confessional context breaks the commandment.

John Bright, the renowned Old Testament scholar who taught at Union Theological Seminary in Richmond, Virginia, was a guest professor at Princeton when I was there. I took his course on Isaiah and remember the gravel-voiced legend saying, "God is holy, holy, holy. He's not just holy or holy holy. He is the thrice-holy God. He is holy, holy, holy. No one nor thing is as holy as God. He is supremely holy!"

He went on to tell us that is why absolute reverence must accompany the invocation of his name. That's why G-D language — "Well, I'll be _____!" or "God _____ you!" — is forbidden. That's why saying anything less than the truth about God as exemplified in Jesus and explained in the Bible is "wrongful use of the name of the Lord your God." That's when God's name is taken in vain.

John Calvin commented on the commandment this way (*Institutes of the Christian Religion*, 1536):

23

It means in brief that we are not to profane his name by treating it contemptuously or irreverently ... We must ... diligently observe the three following points: First, whatever our mind conceives of God, whatever our tongue utters, should savor his excellence, match the loftiness of his sacred name, and lastly, serve to glorify his greatness. Secondly, we should not rashly or perversely abuse his Holy Word and worshipful mysteries either for the sake of our own ambition, or greed, or amusement; but, as they bear the dignity of his name imprinted upon them, they should ever be honored and prized among us. Finally, we should not defame or detract from his works, as miserable men are wont abusively to cry out against him; but whatever we recognize as done by him we should speak of with praise of his wisdom, righteousness, and goodness. That is what it means to hallow God's name.

I was tricked into a debate on a very controversial moral issue about ten years ago in Winston-Salem, North Carolina. The pastor of a neighboring church was at odds with his session and most of the church members over the issue. It was getting very nasty in a Christian kind of way. So he called and asked if I'd come and talk to the session, expecting me to explain that it's possible to disagree agreeably. I guess he picked me because I liked him while thoroughly disagreeing with him on just about everything, including the issue. He knew I'd tell folks that it's okay to disagree on everything as long as they agree on Jesus. Belief in Jesus, after all has been said and done, is the bottom line of church membership — the glue that keeps the church from falling apart.

When I arrived for my informal chat with the session, I noticed the parking lot was jammed. I guessed there was a Weight Watchers meeting or something. So I parked in the lot of the neighboring bagel shop. I stopped in and bought a bagel. I wasn't really hungry but I thought it would be kind of fun to walk in with a bagel — if you know what I mean.

Anyway, my fellow pastor greeted me as I approached the door and said, "Change of plans. I decided to open up the meeting to the whole congregation. We can have a little debate."

The place was packed. Tape recorders and notepads were all around. I spotted a reporter from the local newspaper.

And when my friend began reading from a prepared document, I knew that I had been set up.

My friend spoke eloquently. Unfortunately, he didn't say anything about the issue that was remotely related to Jesus or the Bible.

So I stood up and said:

> *My friend has done an impressive job of twisting the Bible and our Reformed heritage to fit into his personal agenda and ideology. But back in seminary, we called this tactic eisegesis, or putting into the Bible what isn't in the Bible. Our task is exegesis, or taking out of the Bible what is in the Bible. It's like Hans Küng said in* On Being a Christian *(1974), the church's agenda must be "to discover what is permanent ... originally meant, before it was covered with the dust and debris of 2,000 years ... This is not another gospel, but the same ancient gospel rediscovered for today!"*
>
> *When my friend respects the example of Jesus within the context of biblical revelation, I'll listen. But for now, his opinion is opinion. It has nothing to do with our Christological, biblical, confessional, or even constitutional heritage. He's just making up stuff to reinforce an ideology masquerading as theology. I'm afraid my friend is putting words in God's mouth.*

I wasn't very eloquent. But I believed what I said.

No, I believed what God said or revealed in Jesus and the Bible.

As happens in most debates in the church, some folks who took my friend's side really began hating me in a Christian kind of way.

I'll never forget one particularly peeved woman who stood up and waved a finger at me screaming, "What if God made them that way? What if they can't help themselves? What if they have no choice? Who made you the master of morality?"

A little younger and a lot bolder, I replied:

First of all, I don't write 'em. I just read 'em. Sorry, but I didn't make up this stuff. And I'm a little hesitant about contradicting Christological and biblical revelation.

Second, morality is not a matter of what feels good. Moral responsibility has nothing to do with learned or inherited behavior. Just because someone learned behavior doesn't make it right. Just because someone inherited behavior doesn't make it right. For example, I've got this defective gene in me that makes me want to smack you upside the head right now. But that gene and feeling don't make it right.

True and false are not determined by anyone or anything but God through Christological and biblical revelation.

Of course, maybe you know more than God has revealed.

Maybe you feel comfortable in the role of correcting God's judgment.

Christians have a Lord and a book. If you don't like it, that's not God's problem or the church's problem. That's your problem.

It's not for us to put words in God's mouth. We're a little too human for that.

It's for us to take God's word and pray and work to make it a part of our lives.

I was in a tennis tournament about fifteen years ago. I was playing doubles. I blistered an ace right down the middle. One of our opponents yelled, "Out!" My partner at the net turned around and said to me, "God knows."

God knows. So do we. It's all very clear in Jesus and the Bible.

One more thing: The greatest truth about God is his love for us. In what Martin Luther called "the Gospel in a nutshell," Jesus said, "For God so loved the world that he gave his one and only Son, that whoever believes in him shall not perish but have eternal life. For God did not send his Son into the world to condemn the world, but to save the world through him" (John 3:16-17).

So those folks who say this is the anti-G-D commandment are right. We don't say, "Well, I'll be _____!" or "God _____ you!" We say, "Well, I'll be saved!" and "God bless you!"

That's the only way to use his name.

4
Why I Go To Church

"Remember the sabbath day, and
keep it holy." (Exodus 20:8)

I met Rus Howard at Princeton. Rus was just entering as I was leaving, though his hairline has caught up to mine in fine fashion.

Rus, senior pastor of Peters Creek Presbyterian Church, in Venetia, Pennsylvania, is a great guy, loyal friend, great preacher, and great pastor. If I weren't pastor of this church, I'd probably go listen to him. He loves Jesus, loves people, and has a genuine sense of humor.

It wasn't uncommon for seminarians like us to worship at Princeton's Nassau Presbyterian Church when we weren't out doing field education.

I'll never forget listening to some guy begin a sermon, "Today, I want to talk to you about joy." He said that with the enthusiasm of someone getting audited by the IRS. It was like listening to Alvin the Chipmunks at 16 rpm. He was a deadening representative of the frozen chosen.

I am reminded of the fellow who visited a church, got psyched during the sermon, stood up, and exclaimed, "Praise the Lord!" An usher rushed to the man and said, "I'm sorry but we don't do that here!" "But I've got religion," the man announced. "Well," cracked the usher, "you didn't get it here!"

It's like the little wiseguy in New Jersey who turned to his mom and said as we began the closing hymn, "Just my luck! Six verses!"

Unfortunately, if you ask most children and even adults why they don't want to go to church, they'll say its boring.

B-O-R-I-N-G!

And in too many churches, they're right! Lots of churches *are* boring.

But lots of churches are trying to spice up worship.

They can use all of the cheap tricks and gimmicks and techno-graphic-whatevers that they want to use but it won't change the atmosphere of worship until the worship leaders and participants get psyched about worship. Style is no substitute for substance. Content is always more contagious than form. For as one old missionary noted, "You can't give away what you ain't got for yourself." It is the *Spirit in people* that makes worship come alive.

I think of the church with rats in the basement. A meeting was called to discuss the problem. A trustee said, "Let's set some traps." A deacon said, "Let's spray the building." An elder said, "Let's call on our pest control expert." So the pastor said, "I know how we can get rid of those rats. I'll just baptize them, give them communion, and then we'll never see them again."

Why bother? Why go to church?

You may have heard about the man who said to his wife, "I'm never going back to that church. Nobody likes me. And I'm sick and tired of all the complaining and distractions from the mission of Jesus." The wife said, "You'll go back to church." "No, I won't," insisted the man, "and you can't give me one good reason why I should go back." The wife said, "I'll give you two reasons why you'll go back to church. First, you know it's the right thing to do. Second, you're the pastor."

That's not why I go to church.

I go to church for the same reasons that have compelled people for thousands of years: (1) God commands it; (2) I need it; and (3) It's the best hope for the world.

1. God commands worship.

God's fourth commandment is clear: "Remember the sabbath day, and keep it holy" (Exodus 20:8).

The sabbath — the day of worship for God's people (Saturday for Jews because, as we read in Genesis 2:1-3, God "rested on the seventh day and made it holy," and Sunday for Christians because, as we read in Mark 16, Jesus rose from the dead "on the first day of the week") — must be holy or set apart for rest from the regular routines of life and religious devotion to him through worship in the church.

The word *sabbat* means "to rest, to cease from work."

The sabbath is a day of rest from the regular routines of life — a stop-what-you're-doing-most-days-for-refreshment-through-recreation-or-re-creation. It's a day for picnics, ball games, tennis, golf, and all of the rest after worship. Or as my dear and late friend Dick Lane used to say, "It's a mental bath."

The sabbath is a day of religious devotion to God through worship in the church with the people of God. "God is to be served and honored daily," wrote Matthew Henry in 1708, "but one day in seven is to be particularly dedicated to his honor and spent in his service."

Here's the bottom line. We worship God because God is to be worshiped. It's like Martin Luther said, "To have a God is to worship him." Or as Dr. Macleod used to pound into our mushy little Princetonian heads, "Worship is what we say and do when we stand together before God realizing in high degree who he is, who we are, and what he has done for us and for our salvation in Jesus."

2. We need worship.

The late Dean Adams taught Presbyterian policy when Rus and I were at Princeton. Polity is a fancy word referring to how we govern ourselves. Anyway, Dean Adams was asked during one class, "Isn't it possible to be a Christian without going to church?" Dean Adams replied without hesitation, "I guess it's theoretically possible to be a Christian without going to church, but I have never met a Christian who didn't go to church."

Among the reasons for going to church which he provided for the *Ladies' Home Journal* in 1917, Theodore Roosevelt wrote:

> *Yes, I know all the excuses. I know that one can worship the Creator and dedicate oneself to good living in a grove of trees, or by a running brook, or in one's house, just as well as in church. But I also know as a matter of cold fact that the average man does not thus worship or thus dedicate himself. If he stays away from church he does not spend his time in good works and in lofty meditation. He looks over the colored supplement of the newspaper ... The man who does not in some way, active or not, connect himself with some active,*

31

working church misses many opportunities for helping
his neighbors, and therefore, incidentally, for helping
himself.

The psalmist outlined the benefits of close communion with God: "He heals the brokenhearted and binds up their wounds. The Lord sustains the humble but casts the wicked to the ground. The Lord delights in those who fear him, who put their hope in his unfailing love" (Psalm 147).

3. Worship is the best hope for the world.

You may have heard about the little mix-up at Atlanta's airport a few years ago. The air controller said, "Pan Am Flight 407, you are cleared to land on runway B." Just a few moments later, the same controller said, "American Flight 36, you are cleared to land on runway B." "Tower," came a frantic call, "this is Pan Am Flight 407! You just cleared me to land on runway B and now you just cleared American Flight 35 to land on the same runway!" After a pause, the controller announced, "Well, uh, y'all be careful now."

Isn't that life? Y'all be careful now.

We're all crashing into each other. And we've got more needs and wants and concerns and hang-ups and problems and twists and turns and ups and downs and inside outs than any human can handle.

I think of the student who shouted to the university chaplain, "The church is a crutch!" The chaplain shouted back, "You're right! And who isn't limping?"

The greatest need in a person's life is the confidence to live triumphantly amid the meanness, madness, and misery of life in the modern world. That confident living is experienced when a person knows she or he will live forever through faith in Jesus. That knowledge doesn't eliminate all of the hassles but it satisfies the greatest need. And that's exactly what we mean when we say Christians overcome their problems through faith in Jesus. That's exactly why worship is the best hope for the world.

That's why we like to see the pews filled every Sunday. It means more and more and more people are experiencing confident living within the context of eternal life. It's like Luke described the early church: "They devoted themselves to the apostles' teaching and to the fellowship, to the breaking of bread and to prayer ... And the Lord added to their number daily those who were being saved" (see Acts 2:42-47).

Why do we go to church? God commands it. We need it. It's the best hope for the world.

A little girl in Washington, D.C., was asked what she thinks about when she sees the open doors of a church. She said, "I think about walking into the heart of God."

Why do we go to church? God commands it. We need it. It's the best hope for the world.

"Aren't you afraid?" a calm little girl was asked by a frightened passenger as the pleasure cruiser was being rocked back and forth during a terrible storm at sea. The little girl replied, "Why should I be afraid? My father is the captain!"

Why do we go to church? God commands it. We need it. It's the best hope for the world.

There's no fear in worship. There's love and hope and wholeness and happiness and joy and eternal security. Our Father is the captain!

Psalm 95's call to worship says it so well (Eugene H. Peterson, *Psalms*, 1994):

> *Come, let's shout praises to Yahweh, raise the roof for the Rock who saved us! Let's march into his presence singing praises, lifting the rafters with our hymns! And why? Because Yahweh is the best, High King over all the gods.*

Why do we go to church? God commands it. We need it. It's the best hope for the world.

5
Hallmark Card Religion

"Honor your father and your mother."
(Exodus 20:12)

Ross Perot has been asked many times over the past five or six years if he feels qualified to be President of the United States of America. Perot has always answered, "Compared to whom?"

Despite the efforts of Hallmark Cards, Father's Day hardly evokes the same enthusiasm as Mother's Day. Quite frankly, I think there's a fear factor in the mix. Personally, I find this gender bias terribly offensive. And I think it's time for all of us to be a little more sensitive to the fragile feelings of dads. Compared to all of the appropriate hoopla surrounding Mother's Day, Father's Day is about as popular as a Republican in Allegheny County or a Democrat among our Retired Reserves.

Be that as it is, we set aside one day a year to honor moms (the major festival of church and society) and one day a year to honor dads (the minor festival of church and society, which ranks right down there with Ho Chi Minh Day in America).

I think of it as Hallmark Card Religion. One day. Considering the investment of moms and dads in the lives of their children, it's kind of pathetic.

I guess Mary Schmich was right in an article for *The Chicago Tribune* (1997):

> *Accept certain inalienable truths: Prices will rise. Politicians will philander. You, too, will get old. And when you do, you'll fantasize that when you were young, prices were reasonable, politicians were noble, and children respected their elders.*

Fortunately, our Lord affords moms and dads a lot more than Hallmark Card Religion. He even has a commandment just for them or just for us in relation to them: "Honor your father and your mother" (Exodus 20:12).

"This, then, is the sum," John Calvin wrote in summarizing the commandment, "that we should look up to those whom God has placed over us, and should treat them with honor, obedience, and gratefulness."

As a parent, I really like this commandment. It's kind of fun to invoke it around the house as necessary.

As a child, this commandment can be a real pain in the heart, mind, and soul — especially when it's invoked around the house as necessary.

Actually, as I grow older and realize someday everybody will return from the cemetery but mom and dad, it gets easier and easier and easier to want to obey this commandment. Or as Mary Schmich wrote, "Get to know your parents. You never know when they'll be gone for good."

My dad has always been a model of Christian maturity for me. He's tough. But under it all, he's also tenderhearted. Just ask his grandchildren. And he'll always be a better golfer than me. Even when I beat him, I know he was, is, and will always be better. Though I wish he had insisted on a few more things from me as I was growing up under his roof, he insisted on enough to provide a solid foundation for the future.

My mom is the most generous woman in my experience. My dad revels a little too much in the tightwad Scottish thing. So my mom gives her children and grandchildren a lot on the side. She always comes through! And if she had it, I'd already be driving a Cadillac and have spent two weeks touring the historic links of Scotland.

Of course, my parents really annoy me at times.

Whenever I play golf with my dad, he asks, "Bobby, why do you play right-handed and putt left-handed?" I always reply, "Dad, you know I can't putt right-handed. I have built-in yips from my tennis days of heavy topspin." Invariably, he'll pause, look at the sky, look at the green, sigh, and say in muttering tones as he lines up his putt, "Well, I've got news for you. You can't putt left-handed either."

My mom asks me to counsel everybody in Wilkes-Barre when I'm home. "But, Mom," I always say, "I'm here to see the family. Can't I just be with the family?" "Okay," she always answers with one of those sighs as she walks off to do something for somebody while saying to no one in particular, "I just thought you'd like to help."

Of course, I really annoy my parents.

I'll never forget the day after one presidential election. Sitting together for a family meal, my dad lamented, "Only six people voted for George McGovern in Forty Fort. I do not want anyone at this table to raise his hand."

And how many times did I hear this from my mom: "You can say you're sorry, but ..."?

I sense we're all relating about now.

Back to the commandment, our Lord expects us to prize our parents and usually obey them.

Most children — especially during those years before becoming legal when they've got to obey their parents — think parents are a pain. It's a part of growing up. Parents are a pain because they prohibit children from doing things that will hurt them while insisting children do things that will help them. That was Solomon's seminar on parenting: "Train a child in the way he should go" (Proverbs 22:6). That's why we are told to train or teach our children diligently (see Deuteronomy 6).

James Dobson explained the wisdom of obeying parents in *Dare To Discipline*:

> *Nature has generously equipped most animals with a fear of things that could be harmful to them. Their survival depends on recognition of a particular danger in time to avoid it. But good old mother nature did not protect the frog quite so well; she overlooked a serious flaw in his early warning system that sometimes proves fatal. If a frog is placed in a pan of warm water under which the heat is being increased very gradually, he*

37

will typically show no inclination to escape. Since he is a cold-blooded creature, his body temperature remains approximately the same as the water around him and he does not notice the slow change taking place. As the temperature continues to intensify, the frog remains oblivious to his danger; he could easily hop his way to safety, but he is apparently thinking about something else. He will just sit there, contentedly peering over the edge of the pan while the steam curls ominously around his nostrils. Eventually, the boiling frog will pass on to his reward, having succumbed to an unnecessary misfortune that he could easily have avoided.

According to Dobson, children "have some of the same perceptual inadequacies as their little green friends." Children often " 'boil' in happy ignorance."

Dobson's point is simple: Parents have the right and responsibility to guide children away from the fires of life so they don't get fried.

Dobson has said a responsible parent will say, "When I tell you to play in the front yard, it's because I don't want you to run in the street and get hit by a car. I love you and I don't want anything to happen to you." Dobson also suggests a little positive reinforcement or behavior modification: "If you don't mind me, I'll have to spank you to help you remember how important it is. Do you understand?"

About ten years ago in Washington, D.C., I heard Dobson explain parental responsibility in a way that I will never forget. He said children walk through life like walking the hallways of school. And as they walk the hallways of life, there are many doors. Some say academics and athletics and music and clubs and church and love and friendship. Others say drugs and promiscuity and alcohol and gangs and the occult. Dobson said parents have the responsibility to lock some of those doors. Parents have the responsibility to keep some of those doors shut. Parents are called by God to be a holy and righteous pain in the aspirations of children inclined to make bad choices.

One of the greatest theologians of our time, Alfred E. Neuman of *Mad Magazine*, once said, "Everyone knows the difference between 'right' and 'wrong.' It's just that some people can't make a decision." Well, most children don't know the difference until they are taught the difference by their parents. And while most children rebel against parental persistence at first, most children eventually prize their parents for doing their job.

Roy Fairchild, professor of Christian Education at San Francisco Theological Seminary, once asked this question, "What would happen if a visitor from Mars came to your house and asked your children, 'Take me to your leader'?" Think about it. To whom would our children lead them? To Father? Mother? Teacher? Babysitter? Day care director? Homer? Al Bundy? Madonna? Marilyn Manson? The answer is they would take them to the ones who taught them most persuasively and persistently and patiently and passionately. If you're a parent, it should be you. For as John Wesley said, "I learned more about Christianity from my mother than from all the theologians in England."

I guess whoever said it all begins at home was right.

Who said that? God in his fifth commandment.

The big assumption, however, is parents are "in the Lord."

Parents are told by our Lord through Paul to "bring them up in the training and instruction of the Lord" (see Ephesians 6:1ff). And when he told us to respect the authority of parents or the state or anyone "just as you obey Christ," Paul was assuming the authorities to be "in Christ" or working and praying to say the things that Jesus would say and do the things that Jesus would do.

The point is that the authorities in our lives — church, state, parents, teachers, and all the rest — must be "in the Lord" to be in charge. People must never forget *who is* the real head of the house or head of state or head of the church: *God in Jesus!*

That's why our Lord's fifth commandment is about always prizing and usually obeying our parents.

I was finishing the course work for my doctorate at Drew University back in 1981. An older doctoral candidate (Dwight White) said something to me as we strolled toward the library that changed my whole attitude about my parents:

39

Bob, you're very fortunate. You still have your parents. They are the only ones who really care about you in this life. They are the only ones who are really happy when you're really happy and really sad when you're really sad. No matter if you're happy or sad, in the good times or bad times, they never abandon you. They always love you and they always want the best for you. I really miss my mom and dad.

That conversation changed my life. It changed my counseling with ticked-off children. Now I say two things to children who are having problems with their parents — children of all ages — and refresh my attitude at the same time:

First, you can't win an argument with your parents. If you're right, you feel like you're wrong. If you win, you feel like you've lost. So save yourself and your parents a lot of heartache. Chill out!

Second, as Mike and the Mechanics sing, "It's too late when we die to admit we don't see eye to eye." So just love them while you have time.

Maybe there's a selfish part to prizing our parents. Maybe it's something like the song in *Pippin* that goes, "God's wisdom teaches me that when I help others, I'm really helping myself." Maybe our Lord uses this commandment to spare us from the pain of not having prized our parents when we had time with them. God knows over twenty years of pastoral ministry have introduced me to children who wished they had prized their parents before our Lord called them home.

Parents will always annoy their children. Children will always annoy their parents. That's life.

But life is a lot easier looking back, living now, and facing the future when we always prize and usually obey our parents.

I don't know who said this but it makes a lot of sense: "The day the child realizes that all adults are imperfect, he becomes an adolescent. The day he forgives them, he becomes an adult. The day he forgives himself, he becomes wise."

The day we embrace this commandment marks the beginning of honest-to-God relationships in the family. That's why God expects more than Hallmark Card Religion from us.

God expects us to remember our parents. Think of the womb, diapers, good times, bad times, awful times, worse times, better times, best times, and any times. And think of the very big love that parents have had for us through all of it.

I guess that's why this commandment gets easier and easier as we age. Maybe that's why parents want time more than cards.

And that's the meaning of God's fifth commandment.

6

Suicidal Situation Ethics

"You shall not murder."
(Exodus 20:13)

When people think about Dr. Martin Luther King, Jr., "I Have A Dream" or "I've Been To The Mountaintop" quickly comes to mind. And while I put recordings of those sermons on my Sony and pump up the volume whenever I need a little encouragement, "The Drum Major Instinct" is my favorite.

It was preached at the Ebenezer Baptist Church in Atlanta, Georgia, on February 4, 1968 — just two months before Dr. King was assassinated.

Dr. King reflected:

> *Every now and then I guess we all think realistically about that day when we will be victimized with what is life's final common denominator — that something we call death. We all think about it. And every now and then I think about my own death, and I think about my own funeral. And I don't think of it in a morbid sense. Every now and then I ask myself, "What is it that I would want said?" And I leave the word to you this morning ...*
>
> *I'd like somebody to mention that day that Martin Luther King, Jr., tried to give his life serving others. I'd like for somebody to say that day that Martin Luther King, Jr., tried to love somebody. I want you to say that day that I tried to be right on the war question. I want you to be able to say that day that I did try, in my life, to clothe those who were naked. I want you to say, on that day, that I did try, in my life, to visit those who were in prison. I want you to say that I tried to love and serve humanity.*

Yes, if you want to say that I was a drum major, say that I was a drum major for justice; say that I was a drum major for peace; I was a drum major for righteousness. And all of the other shallow things will not matter. I won't have any money to leave behind. I won't have the fine and luxurious things of life to leave behind. But I just want to leave a committed life behind.

And that's all I want to say. If I can help somebody as I pass along, if I can cheer somebody with a word or song, if I can show somebody he's traveling wrong, then my living will not be in vain. If I can do my duty as a Christian ought, if I can bring salvation to a world once wrought, if I can spread the message as the master taught, then my living will not be in vain.

Powerful. Penetrating.

When I first heard that sermon, I was prompted to ask myself, "How do you want to be remembered?"

Well, like Dr. King, it's not a morbid thought for me. I know someday everybody will return from the cemetery but me. And I'd like to be remembered by family, friends, and even people who prevented every day from being a hot fudge sundae. If it proves true, I'd like to be remembered like this: "He loved Jesus! He loved his family! He loved people enough to point them to Jesus!"

It makes me think of a few more lines from "The Drum Major Instinct":

I know a man, and I just want to talk about him a minute, and maybe you will discover who I'm talking about as I go down the way, because he was a great one. And he just went about serving. He was born in an obscure village, the child of a poor peasant woman. And then he grew up in still another obscure village, where he worked as a carpenter until he was thirty years old. Then for three years, he was an itinerant preacher. And then he went about doing some things. He didn't have much. He never wrote a book. He never held an office. He never had a family. He never owned a house. He never went to college. He never visited a big city. He

44

never went 200 miles from where he was born. He did none of the usual things that the world would associate with greatness. He had no credentials but himself.

He was 33 when the tide of public opinion turned against him. They called him a rabble-rouser. They called him a troublemaker. They said he was an agitator. He practiced civil disobedience; he broke injunctions. And so he was turned over to his enemies, and went through the mockery of a trial. And the irony of it all is that his friends turned him over to them. One of his closest friends denied him. Another of his friends turned him over to his enemies. And while he was dying, the people who killed him gambled for his clothing, the only possession that he had in the world. When he was dead, he was buried in a borrowed tomb, through the pity of a friend.

Nineteen centuries have come and gone, and today, he stands as the most influential figure that ever entered human history. All of the armies that ever marched, all the navies that ever sailed, all the parliaments that ever sat, and all the kings that ever reigned put together have not affected the life of man on this earth as much as that one solitary life. His name may not be a familiar one. But today I can hear them talking about him. Every now and then somebody says, "He's the King of kings." And again I hear somebody saying, "In Christ there is no east or west" ... He didn't have anything. He just went around serving, and doing good.

Yes, Jesus was the greatest man who ever lived. He was the God-man. He loved everybody. He's the model. He's the man. He's *God*!

Jesus loved everybody and told everybody to love everybody. He preached invitational, inclusive, and unconditional love. He said to seek the highest good for others regardless of who, what, where, or when without the expectation of being loved back. And the people who didn't and wouldn't love like him killed him.

And that's the cost of discipleship: telling the truth even if people don't want to hear it and will conspire to get you for it (see Ephesians 4:15).

I think of a little story told by Joseph Fletcher in *Situations Ethics* (1966):

> *A friend of mine arrived in St. Louis just as a presidential campaign was ending, and the cab driver, not being above the battle, volunteered his testimony. "I and my father and grandfather before me, and their fathers, have always been straight-ticket Republicans." "Ah," said my friend, who is himself a Republican, "I take it that means you will vote for Senator So-and-So." "No," said the driver, "there are times when a man has to push his principles aside and do the right thing."*

But the truth is people who pray and work to be his in all things at all times in all places shelve popularity in favor of principles.

Frederick Buechner put it this way (*Wishful Thinking*, 1973): "A prophet's quarrel with the world is deep-down a lover's quarrel. If they didn't love the world, they probably wouldn't bother to tell it that it's going to Hell. They'd just let it go."

People who pray and work to be obedient to God alone remind me of the new pastor who was asked, "How do you expect to please so many people?" He answered, "I don't. I'm just trying to please One."

Jesus explained, "No one can serve two masters" (see Matthew 6:24).

Or as I often remind myself, "Remember! You're going to live a lot longer with Jesus than anybody else! So get your priorities and principles in order!"

I say all of that as a preface to the sixth commandment: "You shall not murder" (Exodus 20:13).

Certainly, this commandment has become — rivaled only by the seventh (Exodus 20:14) — the most controversial of the ten. For these are the days when it's intellectually fashionable and politically correct to rationalize all of the ways that we're increasingly killing off the human race.

When we get around to this commandment, there's always a lot of talk about capital punishment, war, euthanasia, abortion, AIDS, and so on. We want to know how we're supposed to respond to these issues as Christians. We want to know what Jesus would say and do about them. That's why we always get back to this commandment. And the guidance that we receive from it within the context of all we know about Jesus and biblical revelation is: Christians don't murder.

Unfortunately, confusion surrounds this commandment. That's because some translations of the Bible use the word *kill* while others use *murder*. But the Hebrew word clearly refers to murder. While some may suggest we're splitting semantical hairs, the words *kill* and *murder* are significantly different. The difference is intentionality. Killing is unintentional. Murder is intentional.

For the most part, killing is a reflex; as in killing in self-defense or accidentally.

You may have heard about the old Quaker who was known for being a strict pacifist. He greeted a burglar late one evening, "Friend, I would not harm thee for the world, but thou art standing where I am about to shoot."

Murder is the intentional destruction of human life. God hates murder. That's what the sixth commandment is all about.

It shouldn't surprise us that our Lord is an advocate of life, liberty, and the pursuit of happiness. God likes life. He created it. He created us. In fact, he created us "in his own image" which means we are so important to him that we can enter into holy communion with him (see Genesis 1).

The Father said, "Choose life" (see Deuteronomy 30:11ff).

The Son said, "I came that you may have life" (see John 10).

The Spirit "reminds" us of God's life-giving-and-life-advocating will (see John 14:15ff).

That's why God gave us this commandment. He wants us to protect and promote life with him.

The truth is Christians are always for life.

Think about the great modern saints like Martin Luther King, Jr., Mother Teresa, Mahatma Gandhi, Pope John XXIII, Billy

Graham, and others. All of them chose life over death. All of them recognized the sanctity of all human life.

So far so good.

Most of us don't go around murdering each other. We know the difference between the killing that sometimes cannot be avoided and the murder which insults our Lord and disputes his right to life. After a few thousand years, we've figured that out.

So far so good.

But I'll never forget my son, James, telling me about a friend who had a bad dream many years ago. His friend was sitting on the toilet in the dream. The toilet turned into a monster and swallowed him.

While James' friend survived the dream, James never approached the potty with the same enthusiasm as before.

But when you think about it, there are a lot of toilets in this world turning into monsters and swallowing people. Lots of people turn into monsters. And God doesn't like it. That's why he gave us this commandment. He wants us to flush out those deadly inclinations from our lives.

Getting back to James, he started screaming bloody murder in the car one day. As parents know, children only freak out when the car is traveling 65 m.p.h. in heavy traffic. Regardless, I asked, "What's wrong?" He answered, "Ben is looking at me!"

There it is. That's our issue. He's looking at me!

If looks could kill! They do. And that's how this commandment relates to us.

"This law," wrote John Calvin, "forbids murder of the heart." Calvin was echoing our Lord who said, "If you are angry with a brother or sister, you will be liable to judgment" (see Matthew 5:21ff).

In other words, Christians aren't supposed to engage in those little murdering acts that spite, slight, smirk, sneak, stare, and scar.

Martin Luther put it this way, "We must not kill, either by hand, heart, or word, by signs or gestures, or by aiding and abetting ... Not only is murder forbidden, but also anything that may lead to murder."

I am reminded of football coach Tom Flores who said, "When you say a prayer and then go out and try to rip some guy's head off, it's kind of ... a contradiction to what you just did. I guess that's why, on our team, it's a silent prayer."

Before laughing too hard, bring to mind the person who was just spited or slighted on your way into the sanctuary.

Before laughing too hard, bring to mind the last time you lost it at a meeting.

Before laughing too hard, bring to mind the last rumor you spread.

Before laughing too hard, bring to mind the last time you did something or failed to do something to get even or get over or get ahead of someone else.

If looks could kill! They do. And our Lord says we've got to flush it!

In *Desert Wisdom: Sayings From The Desert Fathers* (1982), Yushi Nomura recounted the story of some church folks who went to an old monk and asked, "Tell us, when we see brothers dozing during the sacred office, should we pinch them so they will stay awake?" The old monk replied, "If I saw a brother sleeping, I would put his head on my knees and let him rest."

Christians don't murder.

If we disagree on the great issues of our day, should we banter and bark about it?

Christians don't murder.

If we don't like somebody, should we still pray for that person?

Christians don't murder.

If the relationship ended long ago, must we still be open to reconciliation?

Christians don't murder.

If we've been hit, do we have the right to hit back?

Christians don't murder.

Why is it so important to love God and be kind to one another?

Christians don't murder.

One of my favorite people in the world lives in Perrysburg, Ohio. Mark is in his mid-twenties. He is an especially pleasant fellow. I can't recall ever seeing him frown or hearing him say anything negative about anyone.

I've been told Mark has a learning disability. He had to work especially hard in high school and college.

During his senior year in high school, he had an assignment that completely stumped him. It was so hard that his parents heard him stomping around his bedroom in frustration. They had never seen their son so out of control and angry. Finally, he stomped downstairs and said to his parents, "I'm having an awful time. I'm supposed to interview a friend and ask him why he likes me. Then I'm supposed to interview an enemy and ask why he doesn't like me. But I can't think of anyone I consider an enemy."

Mark understands this commandment. His learning disability is overshadowed by his loving ability.

Murder is suicidal. It kills relationships. It kills holy communion with God. There is nothing redemptive about it.

That's why Christians aren't deadly.

They're lovely.

7

Torn Between Two Lovers

"You shall not commit adultery."
(Exodus 20:14)

As a pastor and husband, I'm acutely aware every day isn't a hot fudge sundae for married folks. Aside from the bliss, mist, dog-eyed stares, and couch-cuddling to the tune of Elton John's "Your Song," there are days when wives think husbands come from Mars and husbands think wives come from Venus.

You could write a book about it.

That's why I repeat the twelve words that hold marriages together at most weddings: "I was wrong. I am sorry. Please forgive me. I love you!"

Once in a while as appropriate, I even tell the story of the nervous bride who asked the pastor to repeat the order of the wedding service. He explained, "First you walk down the aisle. Then you stop at the altar and we'll sing a hymn." "Let me get this straight," she said, "aisle, altar, hymn."

There are so many songs about love gone sour or blah or dispassionate or pedestrian. There are so many songs about the way we were. There are so many couples who sadly sing along with Gordon Lightfoot, "I don't know where we went wrong but the feeling's gone and I just can't get it back."

Here are some comments that I've heard over and over and over again ever since I was ordained over two decades ago:

> *"We don't have as much fun as we used to have."*
> *"There's no mystery or magic anymore."*
> *"I can't seem to excite her anymore."*
> *"I can't seem to excite him anymore."*
> *"She used to like ..."*
> *"He used to like ..."*

51

"She's not interested in ..."
"He's not interested in ..."
"She said ..."
"He said ..."
"We never go anywhere anymore ..."
"I can't remember the last time we ..."
"I'm starting to fantasize about ..."
"I think I'm distracted by ..."
"I'm not going to wait around forever ..."
"There's so much more to life than ..."
"There's this other man ..."
"There's this other woman ..."
"I still love her but ..."
"I still love him but ..."

I'm hoping you can't relate to those comments.

Of course, when those desires and needs become frustrated, marital anger surfaces and wives and husbands start killing each other not so softly.

I think of Lady Astor who told Winston Churchill, "If I were your wife, I'd poison your tea." He replied, "If I were your husband, I'd drink it."

Unfortunately, it happens. Too many marriages start with love and end in hate. Why? Why do so many marriages go from sizzle to fizzle?

I'm convinced Willard F. Harley, Jr., a clinical psychologist in White Bear Lake, Minnesota, has provided the most articulate and incisive understanding of why so many marriages fail in *His Needs, Her Needs: Building An Affair-Proof Marriage* (1986).

He has concluded women and men have needs that must be satisfied. If the needs are met, the marriage survives. If the needs aren't met, the marriage is in trouble.

Specifically, Dr. Harley believes a man's most basic needs in marriage are sexual fulfillment, recreational companionship, an attractive spouse, domestic support, and admiration. A woman's most basic needs in marriage are affection, conversation, honesty and openness, financial support, and family commitment.

52

As I've looked to Dr. Harley and many others over the years to unlock the secrets for saving marriages, I've summarized the needs of women and men as emotional, intellectual, spiritual, and sexual. If the needs are met in marriage, the marriage survives and gets better with age. But if the needs aren't met in marriage, the needs will be met outside of marriage sooner or later.

Or as Dr. Harley explained:

> *In marriages that fail to meet those needs, I have seen, strikingly and alarmingly, how consistently married people choose the same pattern to satisfy their unmet needs: the extramarital affair. People wander into affairs with astonishing regularity, in spite of whatever strong moral or religious convictions they may hold. Why? Once a spouse lacks fulfillment of any of the five needs, it creates a thirst that must be quenched. If changes do not take place within the marriage to care for that need, the individual will face the powerful temptation to fill it outside of marriage.*

Obviously, there are lots of unmet needs out there. According to Patricia Love, a marriage and family therapist in Austin, Texas, and Jo Robinson, a best-selling author, in *Hot Monogamy* (1995), "Approximately half of all married men and forty percent of all married women have had at least one affair." Or as my buddy Eric Felack says, "Marriage is like flies on a screen. Fifty percent want in. Fifty percent want out."

Again, Dr. Harley sounds the warning:

> *As I've discussed affairs and how they start, I may have offended you, at least a little bit, by using the second-person pronoun. But I used* you *for a specific reason. While most people would deny they could ever get involved in an affair, the hard truth is that, under the right (or wrong) conditions, any of us can fall victim, if our basic needs are not being met.*
>
> *It doesn't take something different or special to fall into an affair. On the contrary, sometimes very normal*

53

> *men and women get involved in one through a decep-*
> *tively simple process. When your basic needs go unmet,*
> *you start thinking, "This isn't right. It isn't fair."*
>
> *Next time you start looking for support and find*
> *yourself saying, "If only I had someone to talk to."*
>
> *From there it can only be a short step to looking*
> *for support outside your exclusive marriage bond. You*
> *don't necessarily go hunting for this person; he or she*
> *just turns up, and you find yourself saying, "Isn't it great*
> *how we can just talk and share together?"*

At this point, someone may want to urge, "Now's the time to hit 'em with the seventh commandment!"

The seventh commandment: "You shall not commit adultery" (Exodus 20:14).

Pretty straightforward stuff. Don't hop in the sack with someone other than your spouse!

Taking the more eloquent route for a moment, the granddaddy of all dictionaries, *The Oxford English Dictionary*, defines adultery as the "violation of the marriage bed."

Simply, the intimacy of sexuality is to be shared within the exclusive context of providentially ordered marriage.

In other words, don't hop in the sack with someone other than your spouse! That's easy to understand.

It's not "You shall not *admit* adultery." It's "You shall not *commit* adultery." That's easy to understand.

But it's not always easy to obey, especially when needs are not being met within marriage.

I remember speaking to a singles group in Lower Burrell, Pennsylvania, a few years ago. Quite frankly, there were some really bitter people in attendance — people who had been burned by unfaithful wives and husbands. And I knew they wanted me to use the seventh commandment against those who had betrayed them. I knew they expected me to judge and condemn and ridicule all of those adulterers. Instead, I began:

> *If you're not meeting your partner's emotional, intel-*
> *lectual, spiritual, or sexual needs, your partner's needs*

54

will be met with *or* without *you. If they aren't getting it at home, they'll get it somewhere else. I'm not just talking about sexual needs. I'm talking about all of the above. Like it or not, your spouse's needs will be met with or without you. And while you are expected by the Author of your marriage to pray and work to meet those needs, those needs will be met with or without you. I'm telling you the truth in love. If you're not working on your marriage, someone else will be doing it for you.*

Then I said this:

The reason many of you are here tonight is because you took your wife or husband for granted. You stopped romancing them. You stopped doing the things that psyched you for each other. You left them to fend for themselves. And they did!

I went back many times. And more often than not, I got around to the same message: Women and men aren't torn between two lovers when the fires burn brightly at home.

The reason some folks succumb to the sin of adultery — I'm not talking about the totally debauched types! — is because the other half of the marriage has been unfaithful to the emotional, intellectual, spiritual, and sexual responsibilities of marriage. Or as we often say, "When a marriage fails, there are at least two people to blame."

So how can we save our marriages?

"The most obvious way to prevent divorce," wrote Dr. Gary R. Collins (*Christian Counseling*, 1980), "is to build stronger marriages — marriages based on scriptural principles and characterized by love, commitment, and open communication."

To put it another way, marriages are saved by loving our wives and husbands. I mean walking the walk as well as talking the talk! I mean praying and working for their highest emotional, intellectual, spiritual, and sexual good. Marriages are saved when husbands pray and work to meet the needs of their wives and wives pray and work to meet the needs of their husbands. Or as Paul wrote:

> *Out of respect for Christ, be courteously reverent to one another ... Wives, understand and support your husbands in ways that show your support for Christ ... Husbands, go all out in your love for your wives, exactly as Christ did for the church — a love marked by giving ... And this is why a man leaves father and mother and cherishes his wife. No longer two, they become "one flesh." This is a huge mystery, and I don't pretend to understand it all. What is clearest to me is the way Christ treats the church. And this provides a good picture of how each husband is to treat his wife, loving himself in loving her, and how each wife is to honor her husband.*
> — Ephesians 5:22-33

It's called mutual submission.

My friend Eric Ritz wrote about a young Wall Street broker who fell in love with a beautiful actress. But before he would propose marriage, he thought it would be wise to hire a private investigator to check her out. The private investigator gave his report to the broker about a month later. The actress had an unblemished past and spotless reputation. The private investigator's only concern was she had been seen around town in the company of a rich Wall Street broker whose business practices and principles were highly questionable.

Just to exercise a little gender equality, there's a story about a little boy who went to his uncle's wedding. While driving to the reception, his mother asked if he understood what had just happened in church. "Well," answered the little boy, "I kind of understand. But I don't know how he's going to stay married to her." "What do you mean?" the mother asked. "Well," the little boy went on, "you know when the preacher asked those questions? Uncle said, 'Yes,' when he asked, 'Do you take her to be your *awful* wedded wife'?"

No one is perfect. No marriage is perfect.

In "Myths That Destroy A Marriage" (preached on March 9, 1997, at St. Andrew's Presbyterian Church in Newport Beach, California), John Huffman observed:

> *The truth is that every couple is going to have some problems of one kind or another. Our problems will be different from yours. And your problems will differ from those of others, of your friends. Whenever you get two people together, given the many differences and family backgrounds, cultural expectations, and finely-tuned differences in individual temperaments, there will be marital difficulties. The sooner you and I discover this truth and put away the myth, the better off our marriages will be.*

And that's why marriages are at risk every now and then. That's why wives and husbands are sometimes distracted and tempted to break the seventh commandment.

Again, the secret to saving a marriage isn't a mystery. When the fires burn brightly at home, women and men aren't torn between two lovers.

Our Lord's letter to the Church in Ephesus (see Revelation 2:1-7) explains how Christians can renew their relationship with the Lord. It also provides the secret to saving a marriage: "Remember then from what you have fallen; repent, and do the works you did at first."

Remember all of the things that made you so passionately in love with each other.

Repent and do them all over again.

Or to borrow a line: the grass is greener where it's watered.

That's God's way of saving marriages. That's how the seventh commandment can be obeyed.

8

Some Folks Are Just Like The IRS

"You shall not steal."
(Exodus 20:15)

Just like the United States Golf Association says, "I really, really, really love golf." It's fun, good exercise when toting the tools, an unconquerable adventure, and cheaper than other kinds of therapy.

But there are some things that are really starting to bother me. It's getting really, really, really expensive. The costs of equipment and play are escalating quicker than the price of a backup quarterback in the NFL.

I went into a local country club pro shop looking for a Cobra 26° utility wood with a firm steel shaft. Though they didn't have what I really wanted, they had another club that I kind of wanted (namely, a Cobra 12° driver with a firm graphite shaft). But the price was in the ozone layer of reality. They were hawking the club for about 200 dollars more than most retail outlets and catalogues. While I know country clubs appeal to our sympathies for supporting the club and pro, who usually get a cut, I also know such price-gouging — stealing — preys on the game's neophytes and enabling spouses of the addicts whose ignorance about the game makes them an easy mark when holidays, birthdays, and anniversaries roll around.

I really can't stand mulligans — that euphemism for do-overs. My daddy warned me about mulligans as soon as I hit my first worm-burner. He said, "If you don't count every shot, you'll never know how good you really are." He said mulligans, gimmes, winter rules in the summer, foot wedges, and all of that delude us from the truth about our playing abilities. He said it's like stealing or taking something that isn't yours.

When Harvey Penick, the late golf guru who gave us his *Little Red Book* (1992), was asked by some students if they could improve their lies and play winter rules because of bad playing conditions, he replied, "Why don't you play golf?"

I've always liked this little anecdote from Mr. Penick:

> *Two proud parents came to me at the club and announced that their young son had just scored his first birdie.*
>
> *I agreed that was a wonderful event and asked them how long was the putt Junior made for the birdie.*
>
> *The parents said the putt was only two feet long, so they gave Junior a "gimme" to assure his first birdie.*
>
> *"I've got bad news for you," I said, "Junior still hasn't made his first birdie."*

Anyone who has ever played the game knows golf reveals character.

John Freeman was right in *Tee-ology: Golf's Lessons For Christians And Other Seekers* (1994):

> *It starts innocently enough. Discovering an unplayable lie, we kick the ball toward the fairway ... Or on the sly we take an extra "mulligan." Or we refuse to count the additional stroke for a lost ball because the rough, in our opinion, is not cut sufficiently. Or we disregard the out-of-bounds marker on account of our philosophical objection to unnatural hazards.*
>
> *Gradually, and probably imperceptibly, we grant ourselves a selective exemption from the rules of golf ... The one thing we improve in the process isn't our game, but the skill of rationalizing, going through the mental contortions necessary to justify our actions.*

Hitting it straight, he concluded:

> *So maybe there is more at stake than we realize when we ponder whether to nudge the ball away from the*

bush or to dismiss the whiff as a practice swing. More insidious than our reducing our score or inflating our handicap is the real sin of building up our rationalizing muscle, making it harder to subdue on the job, with our family and friends, in our religious life.

Then there's Harry Toscano. He really bothers me.

Harry has a hard time with the truth about his game. Instead of recognizing the truth that his game has never been up there with the best in the world, he sued the PGA Tour on July 14, 1997. Essentially, he claims there aren't enough spots in tournaments for guys like him.

Aside from the fact that Harry was never quite good enough to earn an exemption, he's still not quite good enough to earn his way to the Senior Tour. He sounds like the parents of a bench-sitting eleventh grade football player who doesn't understand varsity sports aren't run like intramurals. Or as Dave Stockton scolded:

I'm terribly disappointed that Harry has taken this route. I don't see people rushing out suing the NFL when they are cut on the last cut. Nothing has stopped Hugh Baiocchi or Tom Wargo or Bruce Summerhays. Tell me, who is a good player who has been denied a chance to play on the Senior Tour? It was not created as a gift for a bunch of mediocre players.

Harry is trying to use a lawsuit to acquire what isn't his. He's trying to steal a spot from those who earned it over the years. Instead of thanking God for the opportunity to qualify on merit like newcomers Albus, Gilbert, Landers, Laoretti, Summerhays, Wargo, and so many others, he's looking for a litigious loophole to gain through the courts what he cannot attain on the course.

I've met folks like Harry in every station of life. They want what they can't earn and don't deserve. Unfortunately, they will break the eighth commandment to get it.

I think of a story told to me by Thom Hickling, the publisher of *Expression*. According to Thom, a preacher visited a seasoned member of the church. As he sat on the couch, he spotted a large

61

bowl of peanuts. "Do you mind if I have some?" he asked. "No, not at all," the woman replied. As the preacher got up to leave, he noticed that he had emptied the bowl. "I'm terribly sorry for eating all your peanuts," he confessed. "Oh, that's all right," the woman reassured him, "because ever since I lost my teeth, all I can do is suck the chocolate off them."

Taking what doesn't belong to you is stealing. It breaks the eighth commandment of God. It breaks trust among people. It does nothing to enable one's communion with God.

You've probably heard of Golden Rule Jones. He was mayor of Toledo, Ohio, during the depression of the '30s. He presided at police court every now and then. As he presided one day, a man was brought in and charged with stealing groceries. The man pleaded guilty and offered no excuse except for the fact that he had no job and no money. "I've got to fine you," Golden Rule Jones said. The major explained, "You stole, not from the community responsible for these conditions, but from a particular man. So I fine you ten dollars." Right after declaring the fine, Golden Rule Jones reached into his pocket, pulled out ten dollars, and said, "Here's the money to pay for your fine." Then he picked up his hat, handed it to the bailiff, and announced, "Now I'm going to fine everybody in this courtroom fifty cents, or as much thereof as he happens to have with him, for living in a town where a man has to steal groceries in order to eat. Bailiff, go through the courtroom, collect the fines, and give them to the defendant."

When we take from others what our Lord never intended for us or keep from others what our Lord intended for us to share with them, we're breaking the eighth commandment.

That's why some folks are like the IRS. Or as I saw on a bumper sticker the other day, "Don't Steal! Our Government Hates Competition!"

The Reverend Ronald F. McManus was pastor of Winston-Salem, North Carolina's First Assembly of God for sixteen years. He just accepted a call to become president of EQUIP (an organization for developing pastoral leadership) in Atlanta, Georgia.

Ron was a good friend of mine. I'll never forget the day he said, "Bob, you Presbyterians never get moving on anything. You meet and study, meet and study, and then meet and study some more. Opportunities just pass you by. By the time you make up your minds, it's too late." When I asked how they did it, he said, "We pray and ask God to tell us what to do. As soon as we agree in prayer on God's will for our church, we act."

Tough concept for mainliners.

But churches like Ron's are growing at an incredibly fast rate. While that's kindling for another sermon, it does explain why the old mainline denominations have moved to the sidelines in the past two or three decades.

Anyway, when Ron was asked how big the church should be, he answered, "As long as there's someone in Winston-Salem who needs Jesus, this church isn't big enough yet."

God help — forgive — Christians who don't think and act like Ron. They're stealing salvation from people.

About two years ago, Ron discovered he has cancer. He said that revelation has changed his life. He reflected, "You face life and death and start thinking, 'How can I live the rest of my life in a way that would make a difference?' "

Ron knows the answer. Ron *lives* the answer. Give!

It's the best way to keep the eighth commandment. Because when you're giving, you don't think about taking or keeping.

I recently heard about a teacher in California who told each of her students how she or he had made a difference to her and the school. She gave each student a blue ribbon with gold letters that read, "Who I Am Makes A Difference!"

Then the teacher gave three more ribbons to each student and told them to give them to people who had made a difference in their lives. The students were told to report back in a week.

One of the students gave a ribbon to a junior executive who had helped him with career planning. Then he gave the two remaining ribbons to the junior executive and told him to honor someone who had made a difference in his life.

The junior executive gave one of the ribbons to his boss. Though his boss was notoriously cranky and crass, he had helped the junior executive in many ways. Then the junior executive gave the remaining ribbon to his boss and told him to honor someone who had made a difference in his life.

The boss went home and said to his son:

> *The most incredible thing happened to me today. I was in my office and one of the junior executives came in and told me he admired me and gave me a blue ribbon for being a creative genius. Imagine. He thinks I'm a creative genius. Then he put this blue ribbon on me that says, "Who I Am Makes A Difference!" Then he gave me a ribbon and told me to honor someone who has made a difference in my life.*
>
> *I was driving home tonight and I started thinking about who I'd like to honor. I thought about you. I'd like to honor you.*
>
> *My days are really hectic. When I come home, I know I don't pay a lot of attention to you. Sometimes I scream at you for not getting good grades and leaving your room a mess. But I want you to know you make a difference in my life. You're a great kid and I love you!*

The boy was startled by his dad's openness and affection. He began to cry. He couldn't stop crying. He cried so hard that his whole body shook. Finally, he looked up at his father through tears and said, "Dad, I was planning to kill myself tomorrow because I didn't think you loved me. Now I don't have to do that."

The best way to keep the eighth commandment is to give. Because when you're giving, you don't think about taking or keeping.

Not long after our youth group returned from "Fun in the Son" (a youth conference sponsored by Presbyterians for Renewal), we had a debriefing. We talked about the good things that had happened and how we can improve upon the experience in the future.

I was a little concerned about some of the financial arrangements. Specifically, I thought it was a bit unfair for our church to pay the way for children who are not members of our church. When I asked what others thought about it, my oldest son Ben squirmed in his seat for a few moments and then blurted out through what appeared to be tears forming in his eyes. "Well, if I had the money myself, I'd pay for anybody who wanted to go to a place where they could hear about Jesus and maybe experience him as Lord and Savior."

It's tough when your children are right. It's tough when your children practice what you preach.

The best way to keep the eighth commandment is to give. Because when you're giving you don't think about taking or keeping.

I think of Tony Campolo talking about an apocalyptic moment with his son Bart in Haiti. As father and son walked through the streets, they were followed by young children begging for money. "Don't give them anything," father warned son, "or they'll want all you have." Bart answered, "So!"

The best way to keep the eighth commandment is to give. Because when you're giving, you don't think about taking or keeping.

Yes, some folks are just like the IRS. They don't give. They take and keep. But "God," wrote Paul, "loves a cheerful giver" (2 Corinthians 9:7).

9
Truth Or Consequences

"You shall not bear false witness."
(Exodus 20:16)

Mother Teresa and the Princess of Wales were larger than life and continue to evoke sympathy, curiosity, and affection.

They were different in many ways — age, portfolio, and the celibacy thing.

But there were some striking similarities — indescribable personal magnetism, a charismatic and contagious zest for living, sparkling eyes, genuine humility, and uncommon compassion.

And now they share something even more important — eternal life. The women who were larger than life transcended life and went home at God's call.

Before her tragic death and dramatic funeral, I never thought too much about the Princess of Wales. I've always considered the royal family to be a silly anachronism — not much more than a tourist attraction. I've always thought their unshared wealth is obscene. I've always thought the adulation afforded to them breaks at least two of God's Ten Commandments. But I always felt a little sorry for Diana. She seemed so out of place among the other wax figures in the museum. She was so real.

Mother Teresa remains a model of servanthood for me. She's one of my heroes. I'll never forget when a westerner said to her, "I wouldn't do what you do for a million dollars." She responded, "Neither would I." She tirelessly prayed and worked to protect, preserve, and promote life from womb to tomb. She didn't pass through slums. She got on her knees and labored in them. One of her aides told a friend many years ago as he arranged transportation for the soon-to-be saint, "No matter what she says, tell the driver not to stop. She'll ask to stop and help everybody that she sees in distress along the way and you'll never get to your meeting."

Except for Jesus, I don't know anyone who enfleshed so much love (αγαπη). She said:

> *At the end of life we will not be judged by how many diplomas we have received, how much money we have made, how many great things we have done.*
>
> *We will be judged by "I was hungry and you gave me food to eat. I was naked and you clothed me. I was homeless and you took me in."*
>
> *Hungry not only for bread — but hungry for love. Naked not only for clothing — but naked of human dignity and respect. Homeless not only for want of a room of bricks — but homeless because of rejection.*
>
> *This is Christ in distressing disguise ...*
>
> *The work we do is only our love for Jesus in action.*

She was so real.

Much has been written, said, and speculated about these two women. Dying within days of each other, the world remains obsessed with comparisons and contrasts. There continues to be the previously predicted assumptions and judgments.

The princess was scandalized by the tabloids before her death.

Parts of the church — way left of center elements in the mainline denominations — were particularly and occasionally cruelly critical of Mother Teresa's radical advocacy of the sanctity of all human life.

Well, I'm not going to get into any of that kind of stuff now or later. I'm always ashamed of the conversations and commentaries and coffee table gossiping about who was more compassionate or who will stand the test of time or who accomplished more or who was better or who deserved more media attention in and after life and all the rest. I'm not going to get into those kinds of speculations because I'm not so sure about my assumptions. I know what happens to people who assume too much.

I do know one thing. God loved them equally. God lived, died, rose, and reigns in Jesus for them equally. I know that.

I know God loves the world — everybody. I know God doesn't play favorites. I know God loves everybody equally.

So I've got to be very careful when I talk about somebody else. I don't want to say anything bad or false about them because I may upset their Father.

I thought a lot about telling the truth and silencing unsubstantiated speculations on September 6, 1997, as I listened to Earl Spencer's eulogy for his sister, the Princess of Wales. I was especially captivated and convinced by his incisive remarks on what motivates people to speak poorly of others:

> *I don't think she ever understood why her genuinely good intentions were sneered at by the media, why there appeared to be a permanent quest on their behalf to bring her down. It is baffling. My own, and only, explanation is that genuine goodness is threatening to those at the opposite end of the moral spectrum.*

Later that day, I renewed a deal made with God about nine or ten years ago. I pledged to accentuate the positive in public and address the pejorative in private. I pledged to live within the rules of reconciliation outlined by our Lord in Matthew 18:15-17. I pledged to make the advice of Thumper's mom my own: "If you can't say somethin' nice, don't say nothin' at all." I pledged to pray and work to keep the ninth commandment: "You shall not bear false witness." And I remembered the counsel of Mother Teresa:

> *It is very difficult to give Jesus to the people unless we have Jesus in our hearts. We all should become the carriers of God's love ...*
>
> *Let us always meet each other with a smile ... Never let anyone come to you without coming away better and happier. Everyone should see goodness in your face, in your eyes, in your smile ...*
>
> *Some time ago a big group of professors from the United States came to our house in Calcutta. Before leaving, they said to me, "Tell us something that will help us, that will help us become holy." I said, "Smile at each other."*

... This is the true reason for our existence — to be the sunshine of God's love, to be the hope of eternal happiness. That's all.

God wants us to tell the truth. That's what the ninth commandment is all about. It means lying and slandering and gossiping are out. It means the truth, the whole truth, and nothing but the truth is in.

John Calvin said breaking this commandment is "evilspeaking." He wrote, "To sum up: let us not malign anyone with slanders or false charges, nor harm his substance by falsehood, in short, injure him by unbridled evilspeaking ... hateful accusation arising from evil intent and wanton desire to defame."

Or as my buddy Dr. Paul G. Watermulder told a group of Cub Scouts back on February 3, 1980, in Woodstown, New Jersey: "That means lying is out. Little lies, half-truths, and pretend stories are out. They will not make you happy, because God does not like them. No matter how much it hurts, God likes the truth best."

It's like the time a mother asked Dwight L. Moody how she could help her children to stop fibbing. Moody answered, "Start calling them lies."

This commandment is broken when we rewrite or rationalize away the Ten Commandments to fit into our less than noble moments:

1. *You shall have no other gods before me unless it's a celebrity.*
2. *You shall not make for yourself an idol unless it's really good art.*
3. *You shall not make wrongful use of the Name of the Lord your God even if you're a Pitt fan in Beaver Stadium.*
4. *Remember the sabbath day unless the Steelers are in town.*
5. *Honor your father and mother as long as it pays off.*
6. *You shall not murder unless you're inconvenienced or really mad.*

7. *You shall not commit adultery unless you're really in love.*
8. *You shall not steal unless you work for the IRS or almost any government agency these days.*
9. *You shall not bear false witness unless you're in court or really don't like someone and want to ruin her or his reputation.*
10. *You shall not covet anything except for what you know you should have.*

Again, the emphasis in this commandment is on the truth, the whole truth, and nothing but the truth.

Anything more or less than the truth breaks this commandment, usually hurts someone, and always offends our Lord. That's why Linda C. Loving, pastor of Oakland, California's First Presbyterian Church, said in Syracuse, New York, during our denomination's annual General Assembly meeting (June 14-20, 1997), "The church is called to be a bird's nest, not a hornet's nest; a place where people come to be fed, not stung."

You may have heard about the young woman who wrote home from college:

> *Dear Mom and Dad,*
>
> *I decided to keep the baby. And so that it will have a proper name, Harry and I are going to get married as soon as he gets out. Harry had a little problem with "the law" and he is in right now. But when he gets out, we will get married. We feel this marriage has every chance of success because Harry has learned a lot in his seven previous marriages.*

Turning the page, her parents read, "Ha! Ha! None of the above is true. But I am flunking chemistry and just thought this letter would put everything into perspective."

When I first heard that story, I thought it was funny. But now I have a son in college.

As his son was packing for his freshman year in college, H. Jackson Brown, Jr., retreated to the family room and jotted down

511 observations and words of council for his son. The result was *Life's Little Instruction Book: 511 Suggestions, Observations, And Reminders On How To Live A Happy And Rewarding Life* (1991). Suggestion 115 is really good: "Give yourself a year and read the Bible cover to cover." Here are some of my other favorites: "Compliment three people every day ... Have a dog ... Stop blaming others ... Eat prunes ... Lend only those books you never care to see again ... Avoid any church that has cushions on the pews."

Mr. Brown includes several entries which directly relate to our Lord's ninth commandment:

> *Spend less time worrying about who's right, and more time deciding what's wrong ... Keep secrets ... Remember that all news is biased ... Just to see how it feels, for the next 24 hours refrain from criticizing anybody and anything ... Don't use time or words carelessly. Neither can be retrieved ... Don't gossip.*

You may have heard about the young priest who made regular visits to a young widow. It wasn't too long before rumors began to circulate throughout the parish and community about his visits. The young priest's visits to the young widow became the focus of vicious gossip.

Suddenly, the young widow died. It was discovered she had been secretly sick with cancer. Only her priest had known of her illness. That's why he had visited her so regularly.

Two women who had been especially responsible for all of the gossip went to the priest and said, "We're so sorry. Father, why didn't you tell us?"

"Because," he explained, "it was none of your business." Then he proceeded to give them a scorching lecture on pastoral confidentiality and the ninth commandment.

"Is there any way for us to make this better?" they asked.

"If you're really sorry," the priest sternly said, "take this feather pillow to the top of the hill just outside of town, cut it open, and let the feathers fly where the wind carries them. Then pick up every feather and put them all back into the pillow case and bring it back to me."

"But, Father," the women said, "that's impossible. The winds will blow the feathers all over the place."

Softly and sadly, the priest said, "Just like your words about our dearly departed sister and me."

Terrible consequences follow breaking the ninth commandment. People are hurt. A person's relationship with the Lord is strained.

I'll never forget the meeting in which I was reminded how to keep this commandment.

A fellow stood up and went on and on and on about the down sides of another person. He scorned, slandered, put down, and made up all kinds of stories to get over on the person. He tried to ruin the other person's reputation by lying about the character of the person.

Finally, an older gentleman stood up and asked, "What's that I see in your eye?"

Be careful when tempted to break this commandment! Remember the person has a Father. And before you say something bad about somebody else, stop and listen carefully. You just may hear a word from the Lord especially for you:

> *Do not judge, or you too will be judged. For in the same way you judge others, you will be judged, and with the measure you use, it will be measured to you.*
>
> *Why do you look at the speck of sawdust in your brother's eye and pay no attention to the plank in your own eye? ... You hypocrite, first take the plank out of your own eye, and then you will see clearly to remove the speck from your brother's eye.* — Matthew 7:1-5

Truth or consequences.

Here's how to keep the commandment:

> *Go out into the world in peace; have courage; hold on to what is good; return no one evil for evil; strengthen the fainthearted; support the weak, and help the suffering; honor everyone; love and serve the Lord,*

rejoicing in the power of the Holy Spirit. And may the grace of our Lord Jesus Christ, the love of God the Father, and the Fellowship of the Holy Spirit be with you now and forever. Amen.

10
It's Never Enough

"You shall not covet."
(Exodus 20:17)

"Oh, Lord, won't you buy me a Mercedes Benz? ..."

You don't have to worry about me singing the whole thing. First, I can't sing like Janis Joplin. Second, I remember Dr. Macleod almost fainted when John Omerod sang it in Princeton Seminary's chapel. Third, the last song that I sang in worship generated a nasty note. Fourth, like most honest clergy, I'd prefer a Cadillac. Fifth, it breaks the tenth commandment of God: "You shall not covet."

Coveting is the churchy word for wanting and wishing for what somebody else is and has. While stealing is taking for ourselves what our Lord intended for somebody else or keeping from others what our Lord intended for us to share with them, coveting is wanting and wishing for what our Lord has given to somebody else.

Coveting puts distance between our Lord and us because it contradicts our Lord's will for our lives. And when we put distance between our Lord and us, we decrease the level of happiness, wholeness, security, and joy in our lives. Vernard Eller explained it this way in *The Mad Morality* (1972): "To covet is to want something you can't have (or shouldn't have) and want it so much that the very desire prevents your finding happiness with what you do have and in what you truly are."

We covet because we feel like we're missing out. Or as that great American Alfred E. Neuman observed, "Live within your income and you'll live without worry — and other things." We covet because we feel like we're missing out.

The irony is we miss out on who we are and what we have when we look at who others are and what they have.

75

Breaking the commandment is *practically* ridiculous because wanting and wishing for what somebody else is and has won't change who we are and what we have.

I remember John Robertson, pastor for many years of Belvidere, New Jersey's First Presbyterian Church, telling me about a local businessman who was quite full of himself. He was also quite successful. Every time they'd get together, the businessman would recite the Ten Commandments and then sanctimoniously say, "You know, pastor, I've never broken one of them." This grew a little old with John after a while. So one day after the man's typical recitation, John said, "I know you know the Ten Commandments. And I know you're very successful. I know you're very wealthy. But Jesus said to give away what you don't need. What do you think of that?" And the fellow replied with a straight face, "Jesus couldn't have meant that."

I am reminded of the time John D. Rockefeller was asked, "How much money is enough?" And in a response exemplifying the inability of experiencing happiness, wholeness, security, and joy by wanting and wishing for what our Lord has already entrusted to somebody else, he answered, "Always just a little bit more than I have."

The problem with breaking this commandment is it's never a *one thing* thing. A person who breaks this commandment always wants and wishes for more. It's never enough. And when we always want more, we are never satisfied with who we are and what we have. That's why breaking this commandment is practically ridiculous.

Breaking this commandment is *spiritually* insulting to God. Or as R. Alan Cole concluded in *Exodus* (1973):

> *Ultimately to desire, and to try to obtain, the property of another is to be dissatisfied with what God has given, and thus to show lack of faith in his love. Further, the envy which this encourages will lead sooner or later to hurt of one's neighbor, and thus is inconsistent with the primary duty of love.*

Father knows best. Father knows what's best for us. Father gives what's best for us. Coveting denies this basic fact of life.

There is a simple cure for coveting: look around and look up.

Look Around: Though I'm like everybody else who will struggle with this commandment until the roll is called up yonder, two experiences in New Kensington, Pennsylvania, have helped me to keep this commandment as well as recommit myself to the food-shelter-clothing-compassionate mission of the Church.

I'll never forget the two little girls who passed by our front porch at the start of another summer vacation. I had a habit of giving popsicles and pop to the children in the neighborhood. So despite my continually receding hairline and expanding paunch, I had a good rapport with the children who lived near the church. Anyway, I asked what they were doing for vacation. With unbridled excitement, they gushed in unison, "We're going to Idlewild Park for vacation!"

Even before they left, it hit me. Their entire summer vacation would be a less than ten hours trip to an amusement park sponsored by our church's vacation Bible school.

And people ask *why* we should give to support the mission of the Church!

I felt okay about the church making their vacation possible. But I felt really bad about that being all the church could do for their vacation.

It brought to mind my first trip to Disney World. It didn't take too long before my pleasure was overshadowed by the pain of knowing some of God's children will never get to go.

That's really sad. If I had the money, I'd ...

Then there was Georgie. Every time I think about Georgie, I want to cry. He didn't have anything. His dad was a wife-beater and child-abuser. He's the kind of guy that most decent people would like to put over their knees and spank real hard. He is one of the two most mean-spirited people that I've ever met. Georgie's mom was in and out of institutions. She meant well. But as my daddy always said, "The road to hell is paved with good intentions."

Georgie was frail. He had hearing problems. He always looked malnourished. His clothes were always worn and tattered. His shoes ... It's so hard for me to talk about Georgie without crying.

And yet Georgie had a spark within him which could not be denied. Whenever he'd see me, he'd yell, "Hello, Dr. Kopp! Hello, Dr. Kopp!" And then he'd run up to me, throw his arms around me, give me a big hug, and tell me how much he loved me. He wasn't ashamed to love in public or even around his peers.

When our deacons gave him a gym bag, several teachers at school told me how he showed it to everyone and talked about how generous the people were at the church.

Georgie gave me a present one day. It's a coffee cup coaster made out of yarn and plastic. It's on the desk in my study right now. It's the best coffee cup coaster in the world!

It's so hard for me to talk about Georgie without crying.

When I look around, it's hard to covet.

Look up: Dr. E. Stanley Jones said:

> *Many teachers of the world have tried to explain everything. They changed little or nothing. Jesus explained little and changed everything.*
>
> *Many teachers have tried to diagnose the disease of humanity. Jesus cures it.*
>
> *Many teachers have told us why the patient is suffering and that he should bear with fortitude. Jesus tells him to take up his bed and walk.*
>
> *Many philosophers speculate on how evil entered the world. Jesus presents himself as the way by which it shall leave.*
>
> *He did not go into long discussions about the way to God and the possibility of finding him. He quietly said to me, "I am the Way."*

Quoting a forgotten source, my friend Eric Ritz said:

> *If a man goes to a psychiatrist, he will become an adjusted sinner. If a man goes to a physician, he will become a healthy sinner. If a man accumulates wealth, he*

will become an affluent *sinner. If a man simply joins
the church, he will become a* religious *sinner. If a man
turns over a new leaf, he will become a* reformed *sinner. But he is* still *a sinner. But if we go in sincere repentance and faith to the foot of the cross, we will become a new creature in Christ Jesus, forgiven, reconciled, and* set free to live.

Joy Davidman wrote in *Smoke On The Mountain* (1953):

There is, in the last analysis, only one way to stop covetousness and the destruction of body and soul that springs from covetousness, and that is to want God so much that we can't be bothered with inordinate wants for anything else.

Or as Jesus himself promised, "But seek first his Kingdom and his righteousness, and all these things will be given to you as well" (see Matthew 6:25ff).

Jesus is enough.

When we look up to Jesus, we don't need to covet.

Or as Gary Beets, Missouri State Director of the Fellowship of Christian Athletes, has printed on the back of his calling card: "If we meet and you forget me, you have lost nothing; but if you meet Jesus Christ and forget him, you have lost everything."

Positively stated and experienced, if you've got Jesus in your heart, there's no reason to covet.

Jesus is enough.